SALSA!
SALSA!
SALSA!

75 Superb Recipes

By Crystal Walls
Special thanks
to Lisa Albritton

© Savory House Press
PO Box 11105, Fort Worth, TX 76110
1-800-738-3927 • WWW.SAVORYHOUSEPRESS.COM

Contents

Postres Salsas

Glossary

Working With Chiles

Introduction

Salsa, Spanish for "sauce," is no ordinary condiment.

Grabbing hold of American palates in recent years, salsa has gone far beyond simple tomato-based dips for tortilla chips. While it is still a great snack for the Sunday afternoon football crowd, creative hands have crafted salsas that are perfectly at home at the fanciest dinner parties.

This book is for anyone who likes to cook and is keen on trying something new. Those who have grown tired of conventional salsas will find something worth making — chocolate salsas, fruit salsas, salsas to enliven entrees. Some recipes are what people would expect of a Tex-Mex salsa; then there are those inspired by other cuisines. Most contain fresh ingredients and all are wonderful accompaniments to any meal.

By no means does this book neglect traditional approaches to salsa making. Included are gourmet versions of such favorites as pico de gallo, New Orleans-style picadillo and tomato-and-cilantro salsas. But from there, whole new areas are explored.

Inspiration for some came easily. Others took work. I would walk through a grocery store thinking, "What haven't I used?" Once I happened to spot rhubarb, an ingredient I had not yet tried in a salsa. So I went home and invented a salsa with raspberry and rhubarb.

After the recipes were developed, my friend Lisa Albritton and I prepared close to a hundred "candidate" salsas for taste testings to determine just how delectable they were. Several were bounced. Some were tweaked. Only the very best were kept.

Surprisingly, the comments were consistent, even though our samplers were a diverse group with different tastes. Everyone loved the chocolate salsas, which we served with gingersnaps. This tells us how far salsas have evolved.

My favorite is the Mandarin Orange Salsa With Chipotles (smoked jalapeños.) I love chipotle peppers and fruity flavors. And though I already had a slew of chipotle recipes, I still wanted one that had a sweet-and-smoke combination, and this came to mind. I made a double batch to make sure I would have some left over for my family after the taste test. By evening, all was gone.

So get out your cutting board, sharpen your knives and get ready to open your mind to a world of flavors beyond any salsas you've ever seen or tasted.

Crystal Walls
Fort Worth, Texas

The author is a native Texan and devoted foodie. After graduating with a degree in hotel and restaurant management, she supervised banquet catering at a historic hotel and at one of the oldest cityclubs in the state. She continued to put her creative instincts to work after the birth of her second son by conjuring up the broadest range of gourmet salsas found on either side of the Rio Grande.

Salsas Tradicional

• • • • • • •

Sinister Salsa

This spicy salsa gets more sinister with each added habanero. Season to taste ... with caution.

3 large ripe tomatoes
1-1/3 cup finely chopped white onion
1 or 2 habanero chiles (depending on your heat tolerance), minced
1/4 cup orange juice
1 tbsp. lime juice
1 tsp. kosher salt
2-1/3 cup finely diced cucumber
2-1/3 cup finely diced radishes
2-1/3 cup finely diced jicama
1-1/3 cup finely chopped cilantro
3 tbsps. finely chopped fresh mint

Halve the tomatoes. Gently squeeze out and discard the seeds and juice. Chop the tomatoes.

In a food processor, combine the tomatoes, onions, habanero, orange juice, lime juice and kosher salt. Process until smooth. Transfer the puree to a bowl and stir in the cucumber, radish, jicama, cilantro and mint.

Refrigerate for at least 30 minutes. Keep in mind that this salsa will become hotter the longer it sits. Adjust seasoning just before serving. Serve with tortilla chips or crispy baguette slices.

Hot Kickin' Chile Salsa

A spicy, full-flavored salsa with many traditional ingredients.

2 poblano chiles
2 cups chopped tomatoes (about 1 pound)
1-1/3 cup chopped green bell pepper
1/2 cup finely chopped white onion
2 jalapeños, stemmed, seeded and chopped
3 tbsps. tomato sauce
1 tsp. Tabasco sauce
1/8 tsp. garlic powder
Salt and pepper to taste

In the open flame of a gas burner or under a preheated broiler, roast the poblano chiles, turning them until blackened on all sides. Place chiles in a bowl and cover with a plate, allowing to cool to room temperature. When cool, rub away the burned peel. Stem and seed the chiles and dice.

Combine roasted chiles and all remaining ingredients and stir gently. Just before serving, stir in salt and pepper to taste. Serve warm with tortilla chips, fish or chicken.

Death By Salsa

This delicious, full-flavored salsa
has quite a kick. Be prepared.

1/4 cup plus 1 tbsp. olive oil, divided
3 cloves garlic, minced
6 roma tomatoes, halved
1-1/4 tsp. kosher salt
1-1/4 tsp. freshly ground black pepper
10 habanero chiles, stemmed
1/2 cup chopped cilantro
1/4 cup lime juice

Preheat oven to 500F. In a small bowl, combine 1 tablespoon of the olive oil with garlic. Mix well. Rub mixture onto tomatoes. Sprinkle tomatoes with kosher salt and black pepper. Roast in oven until they turn color, 15 to 20 minutes. Remove from oven. Allow tomatoes to cool to room temperature and dice.

While the tomatoes are cooling, prepare a grill according to manufacturer's directions. Grill the habaneros over medium-high heat until slightly colored, 2 to 3 minutes. Remove peppers from the grill and mince, wearing gloves.

In a medium bowl, combine remaining 1/4 cup olive oil, diced roasted tomatoes, minced habaneros, cilantro and lime juice. Serve warm with tortilla chips or cream cheese and crackers.

Fresh Herbed-Tomato Salsa

Fresh oregano throws a twist into this salsa with very traditional ingredients.

5 medium tomatoes, diced
1-1/3 cup tomato sauce
1/4 cup minced red onion
3 garlic cloves, minced
2 small jalapeños, seeded and minced
1-1/3 cup minced fresh cilantro
2 tbsps. minced fresh oregano
Juice of 2 limes
1 tsp. salt
Freshly ground pepper to taste

Combine all ingredients in a large bowl. Cover and refrigerate. Serve with tortilla chips, fish or chicken.

Sun-dried Tomato Salsa

**A spicy salsa with the wonderful flavors
of roasted peppers and sun-dried tomatoes.**

1 large red bell pepper
2 large fresh tomatoes
2 large dried New Mexico chiles
3-1/4 cups roughly chopped white onion
1-1/2 cups chopped cilantro
1 cup sun-dried tomatoes
1 habanero chile
2 garlic cloves, peeled
2 tbsps. rice vinegar
2 tbsps. lemon juice

In the open flame of a gas burner or under a preheated broiler, roast the bell pepper and fresh tomatoes, turning occasionally until blackened on all sides. Transfer roasted vegetables to a bowl and cover with a plate. Set aside to cool.

In a small skillet over medium-low heat, saute the dried New Mexico chiles until fragrant and pliable; they should have some color but not appear scorched. Remove from heat and allow them to cool slightly. Discard stems and tear flesh into small pieces. Drop chile pieces into a medium bowl of boiling water. Allow to sit, stirring occasionally, until cool. Drain and set aside.

Remove cooled red bell pepper from bowl. Rub away burned peel; stem, seed and coarsely chop the pepper.

Leave the tomatoes' skins intact. Seed and dice the tomatoes.

In a blender, combine the roasted pepper and tomatoes, New Mexico chile pieces, onion, cilantro, sun-dried tomatoes, habanero, garlic, rice vinegar and lemon juice. Serve with tortilla chips, poultry or pork.

Deep South Green Tomato Salsa

A bright, colorful tangy salsa inspired
by the harvests of the South.

1 cup fresh corn kernels (cut from about 2 ears)
4 medium green tomatoes, cored and diced
1 medium red tomato, diced
1 medium yellow tomato, diced
1 red bell pepper, deveined, seeded and diced
1 yellow bell pepper, deveined, seeded and diced
1 green bell pepper, deveined, seeded and diced
4 green onions, sliced thinly
5 jalapeños, seeded and minced
2 shallots, chopped
2 garlic cloves, minced
2-1/3 cups red-wine vinegar
1/4 cup light-brown sugar, firmly packed
1/4 cup fresh cilantro, chopped
1 tsp. salt
1/4 tsp. ground cumin, preferably from toasted seeds
1/8 tsp. cayenne

Preheat oven to 425F. Spread corn kernels in a single layer on a baking sheet; roast in the oven, stirring occasionally, until lightly browned. Remove from oven and allow to cool slightly.

In a large saucepan over medium-high heat, combine roasted corn with tomatoes, bell peppers, green onions, shallots and jalapeños. Add vinegar; stir in remaining ingredients and bring to a boil. Reduce heat, cover and simmer 30 minutes, or until mixture thickens. Remove from heat and allow to cool to room temperature. Cover and refrigerate until ready to serve. Serve with baked sweet potato rounds, pork or poultry.

Italian Tomato Salsa

A tangy, traditional Italian salsa.

1 cup finely chopped sun-dried tomatoes
1 cup chopped black olives
2 garlic cloves, minced
2 tbsps. toasted pinenuts
1 tbsp. chopped fresh oregano
1 tbsp. chopped fresh basil
1-1/4 cup olive oil
2 tsps. red wine vinegar
1-1/4 cup Parmesan cheese
Salt and pepper to taste

In a medium bowl, combine tomatoes, olives, garlic, pinenuts, oregano and basil. Stir in olive oil and vinegar.

Just before serving, stir in Parmesan cheese and salt and pepper to taste. Serve with garlic bread, pita chips, fried pasta or chicken.

Cranberry Tomato Salsa

A sweet, spicy salsa that is great anytime cranberries are available.

2 cups fresh cranberries
4 tomatoes, seeded and chopped
2/3 cup chopped red onion
2 jalapeños, seeded and minced
Juice of 1 lemon
Pinch of sugar, or to taste

Put cranberries in a blender and pulse until well chopped. Add tomatoes, onion and jalapeños and puree until smooth. Pour into a bowl and stir in lemon juice and sugar. Cover and refrigerate for at least an hour before serving. Serve with tortilla chips.

Tomatillo Salsa

A basic, moderately spicy green salsa.

10 fresh tomatillos, husked and diced
1-1/4 cup minced fresh cilantro
1/2 cup chopped white onion
2 jalapeños, seeded and chopped
2 tsps. lime juice
1-1/4 tsp. salt

Combine all ingredients; cover and chill. Serve with tortilla chips, seafood or chicken.

Border Pico De Gallo

A traditional Mexican accompaniment.

1 tomato, chopped
1 white onion, chopped
1-1/2 cup chopped cilantro
1 jalapeño, seeded and chopped
Juice of 1 lime
Salt to taste

Combine all ingredients in bowl, stir and allow to sit for an hour. Serve with tortilla chips, fajitas or chicken.

Traditional Tomatillo Salsa

Contributed by Cyndi Bird
A traditional green salsa with medium heat.

1 pound tomatillos
1 cup chicken broth
1 tbsp. olive oil
1-1/2 cup chopped white onion
2 green onions, chopped
1 garlic clove, minced
Juice of 1 lime
4 tbsps. chopped fresh cilantro
2 tsps. minced jalapeño
Sea salt, to taste
Fresh ground black pepper

Peel husks from tomatillos. Cook tomatillos in salted boiling water to cover for 3 minutes. Remove from water with a slotted spoon or sieve and puree with the chicken broth in a blender or food processor; set aside.

Heat olive oil in a large skillet and saute white onions. Add green onions just before white onions become soft. Pour tomatillo puree into the skillet; stir in all remaining ingredients and simmer 20 minutes. Serve at room temperature with tortilla chips.

Baby Tomato Pico

A colorful and spicy salsa.

2 cups miniature yellow tomatoes, halved
1 cup cherry tomatoes, halved
1 tbsp. fresh cilantro, chopped
1 garlic clove, minced
1¼ cup yellow onion, minced
Juice of 1 lime
2 serranos, seeded and minced
Salt to taste

Combine all ingredients in a bowl. Stir well to combine.
Cover and refrigerate until needed. Serve with tortilla chips, chicken or white pork.

Sweet Southern Pico De Gallo

A sweet twist of a traditional Mexican favorite.

2 cups miniature yellow tomatoes, halved
1-1/4 cup minced yellow onion
1 cup cherry tomatoes, halved
1 garlic clove, minced
2 serrano chiles, seeded and minced
Juice of 1 lime
1 tbsp. chopped fresh cilantro
Salt to taste

Combine all ingredients in a bowl, stirring well. Cover and refrigerate until needed. Serve with tortilla chips, chicken or pork.

Herb Roasted Pepper Salsa

**Fresh herbs add wonderful flavor
to the roasted peppers and corn.**

2 large red bell peppers
2 large yellow bell peppers
1 medium green bell pepper
3 jalapeños
3-1/4 cup fresh corn kernels, cut from 2 ears
1-1/2 tsp. toasted fennel seeds
1/2 tsp. toasted cumin seeds
1 tbsp. fresh lemon juice
1 tbsp. minced fresh basil
1 tbsp. minced fresh rosemary
1 tbsp. minced fresh thyme
Salt and pepper to taste

In the open flame of a gas burner or under a preheated broiler, roast all the bell peppers and the jalapeños, turning until blackened on all sides. Place the peppers in a bowl and cover with a plate. Allow to cool to room temperature; then rub away the burned peel. Stem and finely chop the peppers.

In a heavy saucepan of lightly salted, boiling water, blanch the corn for 1 minute. Drain and allow to cool.

Place toasted fennel seeds and toasted cumin seeds in a spice grinder and pulse until seeds are a powdered consistency.

In a medium bowl, combine roasted peppers, blanched corn, fennel/cumin powder, lemon juice, basil, rosemary and thyme and stir gently. Season with salt and pepper and allow to stand for at least 2 hours. Serve with tortilla chips or French bread.

Smoky Chipotle Salsa

This smoky salsa is a great starter to any meal.

3 large tomatoes, chopped
3-1/4 cup chopped fresh cilantro
3 tbsps. fresh lime juice
1-1/2 tbsps. chopped canned chipotle chiles in adobo sauce
3 tbsps. adobo sauce from chipotles
1-1/2 tsps. ground cumin, preferably from toasted seeds
Salt and pepper to taste

In a medium bowl, combine all ingredients. Stir well to combine. Refrigerate for an hour. Serve chilled with blue corn tortilla chips.

Quick Cactus Chow-Chow

Contributed by Cyndi Bird
A traditional green salsa with mild flavor.

15-ounce jar nopalitos (prickly pear), drained and chopped
1 white onion, finely diced
Juice of 1 lime
1 loosely packed cup finely chopped fresh cilantro
1 pickled jalapeño with seeds, minced

Combine all ingredients in a bowl and allow to sit for at least 30 minutes to blend flavors. Serve with tortilla chips, pork or chicken.

Roasted Poblano Orange Salsa

A hearty full-flavored salsa
with fresh orange juice and jicama.

2 poblano chiles
2 large tomatoes, seeded and diced
1-1/2 cup peeled and diced jicama
1-1/2 cup chopped cilantro
2 garlic cloves, minced
Juice of 1 lime
1 tbsp. sugar
1 large navel orange

In the open flame of a gas burner or in a preheated broiler, roast the poblanos, turning occasionally until peels are blackened on all sides. Transfer to a bowl and cover with a plate to cool.

Meanwhile, in a large bowl, combine the diced tomatoes, jicama, cilantro, garlic, lime juice and sugar.

When chiles are cool enough to handle, rub off the burned peel. Stem, seed and coarsely chop the chiles. Add them to the tomato mixture.

Zest the orange and add the zest to the bowl. Cut the orange in half and squeeze the juice into the bowl. Stir to combine. Serve with fish or chicken.

Roasted Corn Salsa

**A smoky and spicy salsa flavored with traditional
Tex-Mex seasonings.**

1/4 cup unsalted butter, melted
1 tbsp. chili powder
1/2 tsp. cayenne pepper
2 cups sweet-corn kernels, cut from fresh ears
1-1/3 cup diced red bell pepper
1-1/3 cup finely diced red onion
1-1/3 cup chopped cilantro
2 serrano chiles, seeded and minced
1 tbsp. Spanish sherry vinegar
2 tsps. honey
1 tsp. fresh lemon juice
Salt and pepper to taste

Preheat oven to 425F. In a small bowl, combine butter, chili powder and cayenne pepper. Add corn kernels and toss to coat. Spread the corn into a single layer on a baking sheet and roast in oven, stirring occasionally, until lightly browned. Remove from oven and allow to cool slightly.

In a medium bowl, combine roasted corn, red bell pepper, red onion, cilantro, serranos, sherry vinegar, honey and lemon juice. Season with salt and pepper just before serving. Serve with tortilla chips, chicken or pork.

New Orleans Picadillo

A hearty, traditional New Orleans dish.

1 tbsp. vegetable oil
1 medium white onion, peeled and chopped
1/2 large green bell pepper, seeded and chopped
1/2 large red bell pepper, seeded and chopped
3 garlic cloves, minced
1 pound extra-lean ground beef
1/4 cup canned or jarred tomato sauce
1/4 cup sliced green olives stuffed with pimentos or jalapeños
1/4 cup raisins
2 tbsps. white vinegar
1 tbsp. capers
1 tbsp. Tony Chachere's or other Creole seasoning
1 tsp. salt
1/2 tsp. freshly ground pepper
1/4 tsp. sugar
5 eggs, beaten
6-oz. jar pimentos, drained and sliced, for garnish
6 slices French bread, fried in oil, for serving

Heat oil in a large skillet over medium heat. Saute the onion, green bell pepper and red bell pepper until the onion is translucent, 3 to 5 minutes. Add the garlic and saute for an additional 2 minutes.

Add the beef and break it up well so that there are no lumps. Add tomato sauce, olives, raisins, vinegar, capers, Creole seasoning, salt, pepper and sugar. Reduce the heat to low, cover and simmer for 20 minutes. The consistency should be slightly liquid.

Uncover pan and stir in beaten eggs, one at a time; continue cooking and stirring until eggs become scrambled.

Transfer the picadillo to a serving dish and garnish with pimento. Serve with fried French bread.

Orange Tomatillo Salsa

A sweet, slightly spicy salsa.

3 medium tomatillos, husked, rinsed, cored and chopped
1 large navel orange, peeled and coarsely chopped
1 small red onion, halved and thinly sliced
1/2 cup finely chopped jicama
1 jalapeño pepper, seeded and finely chopped
1/2 cup chopped fresh cilantro
1/4 cup fresh lime juice
2 tbsps. olive oil
2 tsps. honey
Salt and freshly ground pepper to taste

In a medium bowl, combine all the ingredients except salt and pepper. Let stand at room temperature for up to an hour. Season with salt and pepper just before serving. Serve with tortilla chips or fish.

SALSAS ORIGINAL

• • • • • • •

Roasted Red Bell Pepper Salsa

Sweet and spicy pecans wonderfully accent the mellow flavor of the roasted vegetables.

2 heavy red bell peppers
2 tomatoes
2 ancho chiles
4 tbsps. unsalted butter, melted
1 cup pecan halves
1/4 cup light brown sugar, packed
1 habanero, minced
3 garlic cloves, minced
2 tbsps. sesame seeds, toasted
1 tbsp. red wine vinegar
1/4 cup chopped cilantro
Salt and pepper to taste

In the open flame of a gas burner or under a preheated broiler, roast the red bell peppers and tomatoes, turning occasionally until blackened on all sides. Remove peppers and tomatoes from heat and place in a bowl; cover with a plate and allow to cool to room temperature.

Meanwhile, toast ancho chiles in a small saute pan (no oil needed) over medium-high heat until crisp but not charred. When anchos are cool enough to handle, remove and discard stems and seeds; using a spice grinder, grind anchos to a fine powder.

Preheat oven to 350F. In a medium bowl, place melted butter. Add pecans and toss to coat. Add brown sugar and ground ancho and toss to coat again. Spread mixture onto a baking sheet, pouring excess liquid on top of the pecans. Bake 20 minutes. Remove from oven and allow to cool; coarsely chop pecans and set aside.

Remove bell peppers and tomatoes from bowl. Rub away burned peel. Stem and seed the peppers and tomatoes and coarsely chop them.

Combine roasted peppers and tomatoes, chopped seasoned pecans, habanero, garlic cloves, sesame seeds and red wine vinegar and stir gently. Chill until needed. Just before serving, stir in the cilantro and season with salt and pepper. Serve with crispy French bread, chicken or pork.

In a medium bowl, place melted butter. Add pecans and toss to coat. Add packed brown sugar and ancho powder and toss to coat again. Spread mixture onto a baking sheet, pouring excess liquid on top of the pecans. Bake at 350F for 20 minutes. Remove from oven and allow to cool. Coarsely chop the pecans and set aside.

Remove bell peppers and tomatoes from bowl. Rub away burned peel. Stem and seed the peppers and tomatoes and coarsely chop them.

Combine roasted peppers, tomatoes, seasoned pecans, habanero, garlic cloves, sesame seeds and red wine vinegar and stir gently. Allow to chill. Stir in the cilantro and season with salt and pepper just before serving. Serve with crispy French bread, chicken or white pork.

Roasted Poblano Salsa

A mild salsa with the mellow flavors of roasted peppers and the crunch of toasted pinenuts.

2 large poblano peppers
1/2 large red bell pepper
1/2 large orange bell pepper
3/4 cup pinenuts
2 garlic cloves, minced
2 tsps. chopped fresh marjoram
1 tsp. olive oil
Salt and pepper to taste

Over the open flame of a gas burner or in a preheated broiler, roast the poblanos and bell peppers, turning occasionally until blackened on all sides. Transfer to a bowl and cover with a plate. Allow the peppers to cool.

In a small saucepan over medium-high heat, cook the pinenuts, stirring constantly until golden brown and and fragrant. Remove from heat and set aside.

When the peppers have cooled, remove from bowl. Rub away burned peel. Stem, seed and dice the peppers.

In a medium bowl combine the roasted peppers, garlic, marjoram and olive oil. Just before serving, add salt and pepper to taste and stir in the toasted pinenuts.

Serve with toasted slices of French bread, chicken, fish or pork.

Pepper Pepper Pepper Salsa

A tangy salsa with the beautiful colors of summer.

1/4 cup white wine vinegar
2 tbsps. vegetable oil
2 tsps. sugar
1/4 tsp. salt
1/4 tsp. pepper
1 red bell pepper, diced
1 yellow bell pepper diced
1 green bell pepper, diced
2 tbsps. chopped cilantro

Combine vinegar, oil, sugar, salt and black pepper in a small saucepan; bring to a boil, stirring until sugar dissolves. Remove from heat.

Combine peppers and cilantro in a glass bowl; add hot vinegar mixture and stir gently. Cool. Cover and chill. Serve with pork or ham.

Portobello-Basil Salsa

A hearty, chunky, slightly sweet salsa.

2 portobello mushrooms
Olive oil
1 white onion, sliced thinly
2 large tomatoes, seeded and diced
2 jalapeños, seeded and minced
3 cloves garlic, minced
1 tbsp. lemon juice
1 tsp. honey
1/4 tsp. white pepper
1/4 tsp. salt
1/2 cup fresh basil, chopped

Heat a gas or charcoal grill to medium-low heat.

Wash the portobellos, pat dry gently and lightly rub with olive oil. Grill the mushrooms, turning frequently, until cooked through but still firm. Cut grilled mushrooms into small dice.

Film a small skillet with olive oil and saute the onions until dark and caramelized. Remove from heat. Set aside.

In a medium bowl, combine grilled mushrooms, caramelized onions, tomatoes, jalapeños, garlic, lemon juice, honey, white pepper and salt. Cover and let stand at least 1 hour. Just before serving, reheat salsa and stir in fresh basil. Serve with beef, chicken or pork.

Autumn Morning Salsa

**A full-bodied, hearty salsa, reminiscent
of large holiday feasts.**

2 tbsps. chopped walnuts
2 cups fresh cranberries
1/4 cup firmly packed dark-brown sugar
1/2 cup water
1 pear, cored and chopped
1/2 Granny Smith apple, chopped
3 tbsps. golden raisins
2 tbsps. apple cider vinegar
1-1/2 tsps. peeled and grated fresh ginger
1 tsp. ground cinnamon
1-1/2 tsps. grated orange zest

Preheat oven to 350F. Spread walnuts on a cookie sheet and bake until lightly toasted, about 5 minutes.

In a small saucepan over medium-high heat, bring cranberries, brown sugar and water to a boil and cook, stirring often, until cranberries pop. Stir in toasted walnuts, pear, apple, raisins, apple cider vinegar, ginger and cinnamon. Continue cooking until apples are soft, about 20 minutes.

Remove from heat and stir in orange zest just before serving. Serve warm with ham, pork, turkey or chicken or with gingersnaps as a dessert or sweet snack.

Spring Harvest Salsa

**Fresh from the garden, this mild salsa combines
all of summer's favorite flavors.**

1/4 pound fresh green beans
2 ears fresh corn
3 tomatoes, diced
1/2 cup chopped cilantro, loosely packed
2 garlic cloves, minced
Juice of 2 limes
1/4 cup olive oil
1/4 cup diced green bell pepper
1/4 cup diced red onion
2 tbsps. minced fresh basil
1/2 tsp. salt
1/4 tsp. freshly ground black pepper

Wash beans and remove strings. Remove husks and silks from corn. Place beans and corn in boiling water to cover. Return water to a boil; cook 4 minutes. Drain and immediately cover vegetables with ice water. Let stand until cool; drain. Cut corn from cob and cut beans into 1/4-inch pieces.

Combine beans, corn and all remaining ingredients, stirring gently; cover and chill. Serve with tortilla chips, fish or chicken.

Black-Bean Papaya Salsa

**Inspired from the Mexican Caribbean, this mild
salsa combines the earthy flavor of black beans
with the sweet flavor of papaya.**

1 cup canned black beans, drained and rinsed
1 ripe medium papaya, seeded, peeled and cut into 1/2-inch dice
1/2 medium red bell pepper, cut into 1/2-inch dice
1 medium jalapeño, seeded and finely chopped
1 medium green onion, minced
1-1/2 tbsps. fresh lime juice
1 tbsp. olive oil
1-1/2 tsps. rice wine vinegar
1-1/2 tsps. peeled and minced fresh ginger
1/2 tsp. sugar
1/2 tsp. kosher salt
Dash of cayenne pepper
1 tbsp. minced fresh cilantro

In a large bowl, combine the black beans, papaya, red bell pepper,
jalapeño and green onion.

In a small bowl, combine the lime juice, oil, vinegar, ginger, sugar,
salt and cayenne. Fold this mixture into the beans. Refrigerate for up
to 6 hours.

Just before serving, stir in the cilantro and serve chilled with chick-
en, fish or pork.

Fruited Cactus Salsa
Oranges and cherries make this salsa as beautiful as it is delicious.

2 cactus pads (nopales), thorns and bristles removed (see note)
2 tbsps. unsalted butter, melted
Salt and pepper to taste
3 oranges, peeled, sectioned, membranes removed
2 cups stemmed, pitted and coarsely chopped fresh cherries
1/2 cup chopped fresh cilantro
1 chipotle pepper in adobo sauce, pureed in blender
Juice from 1 medium orange
1 tbsp. white wine vinegar
1/2 tsp. salt

Preheat a grill.

Cut each cactus pad into a "fan" by making several vertical cuts about 1/4 inch apart, starting from the top of the pad and leaving about 2 inches of the base intact. Brush each pad with butter and season with salt and pepper.

Grill cactus over medium heat until charred and soft. Allow to cool and then cut across the pads where slits end to free the cactus strips. Stack the strips and cut into 1 1/2-inch sections.

In a medium bowl, combine grilled cactus, orange sections, chopped cherries and cilantro.

In a small bowl, combine chipotle puree, orange juice, vinegar and salt. Add to the grilled cactus mixture and stir to combine. Serve at room temperature with tortilla chips, crackers, pork, chicken or turkey.

NOTE: Most Hispanic markets sell whole prickly-pear pads with thorns already removed.

Steamin' Carrot Salsa

Sweet carrots are given a bite in this moderately spicy salsa.

1 bunch green onions, minced
1 cup finely chopped carrot
1 large tomato, seeded and chopped
2 garlic cloves, minced
1 habanero pepper, seeded and chopped
3 tbsps. chopped cilantro
1 tbsp. lime juice
Salt to taste

In a medium bowl, combine onions, carrot, tomato and garlic. Refrigerate until needed.

Just before serving, add habanero, cilantro, lime juice and salt to taste. Serve immediately with tortilla chips, crackers or fish.

Sweet & Spicy Onion Salsa

**More sweet than spicy. This grilled salsa
is sure to be a favorite.**

2 pounds sweet yellow onions (1015s or Vidalia)
¼ cup olive oil
3 tbsps. apple cider vinegar
2 tbsps. packed light-brown sugar
1/4 tsp. cayenne pepper
Salt and freshly ground pepper to taste

Preheat a grill.

Peel the onions and slice them crosswise in rings about 1/2-inch thick. Toss the onion rings with olive oil to lightly coat and place on the grill over low heat; brush onions with oil once or twice during cooking. When onions are tender and charred (about 20 minutes), remove from grill and allow to cool slightly. Dice the onions and transfer to large bowl.

In a small nonreactive saucepan, bring the vinegar and brown sugar to a simmer over low heat. Stir the mixture occasionally until the sugar has dissolved, about 3 minutes.

Pour the mixture over the onions and season with cayenne, salt and pepper.

Serve warm or at room temperature with pork, beef or chicken, or as an accompaniment for burgers.

Grecian Island Salsa

Contributed by Cyndi Bird
A mild salsa full of robust flavor.

14-oz. can black olives, chopped
1 cup minced fresh parsley
4 oz. feta cheese, crumbled
1/2 cup minced white onion
Juice of 1 lime
2 tbsps. olive oil
2 tbsps. minced fresh dill
Freshly ground black pepper to taste

Combine all ingredients and stir gently. Serve immediately with toasted baguette slices or pita chips.

Greek Goddess Salsa

A mild, creamy salsa inspired by the Aegean Islands.

3 large tomatoes, divided
4 garlic cloves, divided
1/2 cup chopped white onion
1/4 cup commercial Caesar dressing
1/4 cup sliced black olives
2 tbsps. stemmed and minced peperoncini
1 tsp. lemon juice
1/4 tsp. white pepper
1/2 cup crumbled feta cheese
1 tbsp. chopped fresh basil

In a blender, combine half of one of the tomatoes, 3 of the garlic cloves, the chopped onion and Caesar dressing. Process until smooth and set aside.

Dice remaining 2-1/2 tomatoes and mince remaining garlic clove. In a large bowl, combine diced tomatoes, minced garlic, black olives, peperoncini, lemon juice and white pepper. Add the Caesar dressing mixture and stir to blend. Cover and refrigerate until ready to use.

Just before serving, stir in basil and feta cheese. Serve chilled with crackers, pita chips or chicken.

Thailand Dreamin' Salsa

A slightly sweet and very fresh-tasting salsa. Inspired by delicious Thai cuisine.

4 medium cucumbers, peeled, seeded and coarsely chopped
1 red bell pepper, seeded and diced
½ cup chopped sweet yellow onion
1 tsp. salt
2 tbsps. plus 1 tsp. sugar, divided
1/2 cup coarsely crushed dry-roasted peanuts
2 tbsps. smooth peanut butter
2 tbsps. hoisin sauce
2 tbsps. water
2 tbsps. rice vinegar
1 to 2 tbsps. crushed red pepper flakes, to taste
1 tbsp. ketchup
2 tbsps. fresh mint
1/3 cup chopped fresh basil
1/3 cup chopped fresh cilantro

In a medium bowl, combine cucumbers, bell pepper, onion, salt and 2 tbsps. of the sugar. Allow to sit at room temperature for 30 minutes.

In a small bowl, whisk together the peanuts, peanut butter, hoisin sauce, water, rice vinegar, pepper flakes, ketchup, remaining 1 tsp. sugar and fresh mint. Stir this mixture into the cucumber mixture. Cover and chill.

Just before serving, stir in the basil and cilantro. Serve with Asian rice crackers or pork.

Smokin' Gun Western Salsa

This smoky, hearty salsa is inspired by flavors found in some of Texas' best barbecue joints.

2 tbsps. unsalted butter, melted
2 tbsps. chili powder
Grated zest of 1 lime
1 tbsp. fresh lime juice
1/4 tsp. paprika
1/8 tsp. cayenne pepper
2 ears corn, husks and silks removed
1 whole head garlic
1 tsp. olive oil
Leaves from 1 sprig thyme
1 large red onion, cut into wedges
2 large tomatoes
Liquid smoke for basting
1/2 cup smoky commercial barbecue sauce
2 jalapeños, seeded and minced
2 roma tomatoes, seeded and diced
1/2 cup chopped cilantro

In a small bowl, mix butter, chili powder, lime zest and juice, paprika and cayenne until blended and smooth. Spread butter mixture on ears of corn and then wrap each ear in aluminum foil. Refrigerate up to 3 hours.

In the meantime, preheat oven to 350F. Peel away any excess papery skin from the garlic head. Slice off the very top of the head so that the cloves are exposed. Drizzle with olive oil and sprinkle with thyme. Wrap the garlic tightly in foil and bake for 1 hour, or until garlic is soft and aromatic.

Allow the garlic to cool slightly. Gently squeeze the cloves out of their peeling and mash them with a fork. Measure out 1 tbsp. of mashed garlic and set aside (save remainder for another use).

Turn oven up to broil. Place onion and tomatoes on baking sheet and baste with liquid smoke. Roast, turning occasionally, until tomato skins are blackened. Place tomatoes in a large bowl and cover with a plate; allow to sit for at least 20 minutes to loosen skins. Meanwhile, coarsely dice the onion wedges. When tomatoes are cool, rub away the burned tomato skin and coarsely dice the tomatoes.

Prepare a grill according to manufacturer's directions. Remove foil-wrapped corn from fridge and grill for 10 to 15 minutes, or until tender, turning once or twice. Remove from heat and unwrap foil. When cool enough to handle, cut corn kernels from cob and set aside. Discard bare cobs.

In a large bowl, combine grilled corn, the tablespoon of roasted garlic, chopped roasted onion and tomatoes. Stir in barbecue sauce, jalapeños, roma tomatoes and cilantro. Serve with tortilla chips, chicken, brisket or pork.

Backyard Barbecue Salsa

This smoky salsa brings the flavor of the great outdoors to your kitchen.

1/2 cup smoky barbecue sauce
1/2 cup ketchup
1/4 cup Jack Daniel's whiskey
2 tbsps. apple cider vinegar
1-1/2 tsps. Tabasco sauce
15-oz. can black beans, rinsed and drained
15-oz. can Green Giant Mexicorn, drained
1 large red onion, finely chopped
2 large tomatoes, seeded and cut into small dice
4 green onions, chopped
3 cloves garlic, minced

In a large bowl, combine barbecue sauce, ketchup, whiskey, vinegar and Tabasco and stir well. Add the remaining ingredients and stir to combine.

Serve warm or chilled with hot bread or crackers or as a topping for barbecued meat.

Honey-Mustard Salsa

A very sweet and chunky salsa.

1/4 cup mayonnaise
1 tbsp. yellow mustard
1 tbsp. white vinegar
1 tbsp. honey
1 tbsp. finely chopped white onion
Pinch of salt
Pinch of sugar
1/4 cup oil
1/2 pound bacon, cooked and chopped
4 roma tomatoes, coarsely chopped
1 bunch green onions, chopped
1 avocado, peeled and diced

In a large bowl, combine mayonnaise, mustard, vinegar, honey, onion, salt and sugar. Stir well to combine. While stirring, add oil in a slow, steady stream. Stir to blend well. Add bacon, tomatoes and green onions, stirring gently.

Just before serving, stir in avocado. Serve warm or at room temperature with chicken or pork.

Hot Blue Cheese Salsa

A tangy salsa that combines traditional salsa flavors with the hearty flavor of blue cheese.

1 medium red bell pepper
3 large tomatoes, seeded and diced
1 white onion, diced
3 cloves garlic, minced
1/2 cup red wine vinegar
1 tbsp. coarsely ground black pepper
1/2 cup crumbled blue cheese
Salt to taste

In the open flame of a gas burner or under a preheated broiler, roast the bell pepper, turning occasionally until blackened on all sides. Remove from heat and place in a medium bowl. Cover with a plate and allow to cool for 20 minutes. Rub off the burned peel; stem, seed and coarsely chop pepper.

In a medium saucepan over low heat, combine the chopped bell pepper, tomatoes, onion, garlic, vinegar and black pepper. Cook until just heated through.

Pour into a serving dish. Stir in blue cheese and season with salt.

Serve warm with baked potato rounds, pita chips or crackers.

Orange Infused Shrimp Salsa

Inspired by the Yucatan, this sweet, hearty salsa would traditionally be served with popcorn.

1 large tomato
1 yellow bell pepper
1/2 white onion, unpeeled
2 pounds medium shrimp, peeled, deveined and coarsely chopped
2 jalapeños, seeded and chopped
3/4 cup fresh lime juice
1/2 cup fresh orange juice
Salt to taste
1 red onion, sliced into thin strips
1/2 cup peeled and diced jicama
1/4 cup tomato juice
1/4 cup finely chopped fresh cilantro
2 tbsps. finely chopped green onions
2 tbsps. finely chopped chives
1 tbsp. sugar
Tabasco sauce to taste
1/2 cup dry roasted peanuts, chopped

In the open flame of a gas burner or under a preheated broiler, roast the tomato, yellow bell pepper and onion, turning occasionally until blackened on all sides. Transfer to a large bowl and cover with a plate. Allow to cool. Peel, stem and seed the bell pepper and peel the onion. Chop all the roasted vegetables into medium dice.

Place a large bowl of ice water near the stove. Fill a large pot with water, cover and bring to a boil. Reduce heat to medium-high. Add shrimp and cook for about 30 seconds — just to blanch. Remove shrimp with a slotted spoon or large sieve and immediately place in a bowl of ice water to stop cooking process. Drain the shrimp and allow to dry thoroughly.

In a blender, combine the roasted tomato, bell pepper and onion with the jalapeños, lime juice and orange juice and process until smooth. Transfer to a large bowl and add the shrimp. Season with salt to taste. Stir in the red onion, jicama, tomato juice, cilantro, green onions, chives, sugar and Tabasco. Cover and refrigerate for at least 2 hours.

Just before serving, stir in the peanuts. Serve with crusty French bread on the side and pass bowls of unsalted popcorn and corn nuts.

Warm Onion Salsa

A sweet and tangy salsa with a just a hint of fresh rosemary.

1 tbsp. olive oil
5 cups red onion, cut into slivers
1/4 cup sugar
2 tbsps. red wine vinegar
2 tsps. chopped fresh rosemary
1/4 tsp. salt
1/4 tsp. pepper

In a large non-stick skillet over medium-high heat, warm olive oil. Add onions and saute until lightly browned. Add sugar, vinegar, rosemary, salt and pepper. Reduce heat to medium and simmer for an additional 5 minutes. Serve warm with water crackers, chicken, turkey or fish, or as an accompaniment for sandwiches and burgers.

Shrimp Baby Shrimp Salsa

A mild, full-flavored salsa.

2 (16-oz.) packages frozen precooked baby salad shrimp
3 large tomatoes, seeded and diced
3 cloves garlic, minced
1 fresh poblano pepper, stemmed, seeded and finely chopped
4 green onions, chopped
1/2 cup minced cilantro
Juice of 2 limes
1/4 tsp. white pepper
1/2 tsp. chili powder
Salt to taste
1/2 cup grated Parmesan cheese

Defrost shrimp according to package directions. In a medium bowl, combine shrimp, tomatoes, garlic, poblano, onions, cilantro, lime juice, white pepper, chili powder and salt.

Just before serving, stir in the Parmesan cheese. Serve with crusty bread or crackers.

Ceviche Salsa

Inspired from a favorite coastal Mexican dish, this salsa has the mild fresh taste of the sea.

1 fillet of whitefish
Enough lime juice to cover fish
6 roma tomatoes, divided
3/4 cup finely chopped white onion, divided
2 cloves garlic, chopped
1 tbsp. fresh lime juice
Tabasco sauce, to taste
1/2 cup chopped fresh cilantro
1 avocado, peeled and chopped

In a nonreactive dish, combine whitefish and lime juice. Refrigerate 6 to 8 hours, allowing the lime juice to "cook" the fish.

In a blender, combine 3 of the tomatoes, ½ cup of the onion, garlic, lime juice and Tabasco and process to a salsa consistency. Pour into a large bowl.

Remove marinated fish from refrigerator and cut into small dice. Stir into tomato mixture. Return to refrigerator until needed.

Just before serving, dice remaining 3 tomatoes and stir them into the ceviche, along with the cilantro, avocado and remaining 1/4 cup chopped onion. Serve well chilled with crackers, slices of French bread or toasted tortillas.

Avocado Salsa With Crab

A slightly sweet, mild salsa with great texture.

1 large tomato, diced
1 small white onion, chopped
16-oz. can lump crabmeat
14-oz. can chopped green chiles, undrained
1 clove garlic, minced
1/2 cup chopped cilantro, firmly packed
1/3 cup white wine vinegar
2 tbsps. water
1 tbsp. honey
3/4 tsp. salt
1/2 tsp. ground cumin, preferably from toasted seeds
1/4 tsp. pepper
2 ripe avocados, peeled and diced

Combine all ingredients except avocados. Stir well. Cover and refrigerate.

Just before serving, add avocados and stir gently. Serve with tortilla chips, chicken or seafood.

Smoked Salmon Salsa

**A tangy salsa heavily flavored with delicious
smoked salmon.**

1 large tomato
1-1/2 cups chopped yellow onion, divided
2 tbsps. fresh lemon juice
6 oz. smoked salmon, flaked
2 roma tomatoes, diced
1/4 cup capers, drained
2 tbsps. chopped fresh dill

In the open flame of a gas burner or under a preheated broiler, roast the tomato, turning occasionally, until blackened on all sides. Transfer to a bowl and cover with a plate. Allow to cool; peel and chop the tomato, removing as many seeds as possible.

In a blender, combine the roasted tomato, 1/4 cup of the yellow onion and the lemon juice. Puree until smooth. Pour into a medium bowl and add the smoked salmon, remaining 1/4 cup yellow onion, diced roma tomatoes and capers. Stir well to combine. Cover and refrigerate until ready to use.

Just before serving, stir in fresh dill. Serve with crackers, bagel chips or tortilla chips.

SALSAS DE FRUTAS
• • • • • • •

Mango-Peach Salsa

A traditional fruit salsa that is mild and sweet.

Large red bell pepper
Large mango, peeled, pitted and diced
Large peach, peeled and diced
1/2 cup minced red onion
2 plum tomatoes, seeded and diced
1/2 serrano chile, minced
Juice of 1 lime
2 tbsps. fresh orange juice
1 tbsp. mined fresh cilantro
1/4 tsp. finely grated orange zest
Salt and freshly ground pepper to taste

In the open flame of a gas burner or under a preheated broiler, roast the red bell pepper, turning occasionally, until blackened on all sides. Transfer to a bowl and cover with a plate. Allow to cool to room temperature. Rub away the burned peel; stem, seed and dice the bell pepper.

Combine bell pepper and remainding ingredients in a bowl and stir. Allow to stand for an hour before serving. Serve with tortilla chips, fish or pork.

Barbecue Mango Salsa

**A sweet and smoky salsa that is as
full-flavored as it is beautiful.**

Dried pasilla chile, stemmed, slit and seeded
Large mango, peeled, pitted and diced
Medium red onion, peeled and chopped
1 cup peeled and diced jicama
2 cloves garlic, minced
2 tbsps. chopped fresh cilantro
2 serrano chiles, stemmed, seeded and minced
1/4 cup apple cider vinegar
Juice of 2 limes
Juice of 1 navel orange
Zest of 1 navel orange
1 tbsp. light-brown sugar
1 tbsp. cornstarch
1 tbsp. dry mustard
1 tbsp. Dijon mustard
Salt to taste

In a small dry skillet over medium-high heat, heat the pasilla chile for 30 seconds to 2 minutes, until it begins to puff up. Transfer chile to a bowl and submerge in warm water. Allow chile to stand in water for 30 minutes. When chile is rehydrated, strain it, reserving the liquid. Place the chile in a blender and puree to a thick paste. (If needed, add just enough of the soaking water to make pureeing possible.) Strain the puree through a sieve. Set aside.

In a medium bowl, combine the mango, onion, jicama, garlic, cilantro and serranos. Stir to combine. Set aside.

In a medium saucepan over medium-low heat, combine the pasilla puree, vinegar, lime juice, orange juice, orange zest, brown sugar, cornstarch, dry mustard and Dijon mustard. Cook, stirring frequently until sugar is melted and sauce is thickened. Pour over mango mixture and toss to combine; add salt to taste. Serve warm or chilled with tortilla chips, crackers, fish or poultry.

Polynesian Salsa

This salsa combines many favorite flavors of the Pacific to create a fruity salsa with a little kick.

1/2 cup fresh pineapple chunks
1/2 cup diced fresh mango
1/2 cup diced papaya
1/2 cup chopped canned Mandarin oranges
1/2 cup chopped red onions
1/2 cup canned black beans, rinsed and drained
1 jalapeño, minced

Combine all ingredients. Allow to sit for at least 30 minutes. Serve with chicken or fish.

What a Peach! Salsa

A sweet, slightly spicy salsa with a touch of fresh mint.

5 ripe, sweet peaches, peeled and chopped, divided
1/2 tsp. peeled and minced fresh ginger
1/4 cup green onions, minced
1-1/2 tbsps. sugar
1-1/2 tbsps. fresh lime juice
1/2 tsp. dry mustard
1/8 tsp. salt
1/8 tsp. white pepper
1 tbsp. chopped mint

Combine 1/4 of peaches with ginger in a blender. Process until smooth. Pour into a bowl and add remaining ingredients except mint. Stir gently. Cover and chill up to 4 hours. Just before serving, stir in fresh mint. Serve with ham, pork, chicken or seafood.

Bourbon-Peach Salsa

This sweet, spiked salsa is wonderful to serve
on a hot summer afternoon.

4 large, sweet peaches, peeled and diced
1/2 cup sugar
1/3 cup bourbon
2 tbsps. honey
1-1/2 tsps. minced fresh ginger
Juice of 1 lime
Zest of 1 lime

In a large nonreactive bowl, combine diced peaches, sugar and bourbon. Cover and refrigerate at least 3 hours before draining peaches and reserving 1/4 cup of liquid.

In a serving bowl, add the 1/4 cup of liquid back to the marinated peaches and stir in the honey, ginger, lime juice and lime zest. Serve chilled or warm with chicken, fish or seafood.

Caribbean Sun Salsa

A very sweet salsa with a bit of an afterbite.

1/2 cup dark rum
1/3 cup packed dark-brown sugar
1/4 cup lime juice
1 habanero chile
1 cup fresh pineapple chunks
4 passion fruit, peeled and diced
1/2 cup canned mandarin oranges

In a blender, combine the rum, brown sugar, lime juice and habanero. Process until smooth.

In a medium bowl, combine the pineapple, passion fruit and oranges. Pour the rum mixture over the fruit and stir to combine.

Serve with toasted Hawaiian bread, pork or chicken.

Island Passion Salsa

Traditional Hawaiian ingredients and Beaujolais give this salsa a wonderful dessert flavor.

1 cup flaked coconut
1 cup Beaujolais or other fruity wine
2 tbsps. fresh lime juice
2 tbsps. honey
1/2 cup peeled, pitted and diced mango
1/2 cup peeled and diced papaya
2 bananas, peeled and diced
1/2 cup diced honeydew melon flesh
1/2 cup macadamia nuts, crushed

In a small skillet over medium heat, toast the coconut, stirring frequently until browned. Remove from heat and set aside.

In a small bowl, stir together wine, lime juice and honey until thoroughly combined. Set aside

In a serving dish, combine the mango, papaya, bananas, melon and macadamia nuts. Add the toasted coconut and the wine mixture and stir well to combine. Allow to sit for an hour; serve chilled.

Watermelon Salsa

A colorful and delicious fruit salsa.

2 cups seeded and cubed watermelon
1 cup peeled and cubed peaches
3 jalapeño peppers, seeded and minced
3/4 cup finely chopped purple onion
1/2 cup finely chopped fresh cilantro
2 tbsps. fresh lime juice
1 tsp. grated orange zest
1/2 tsp. salt

Stir together all ingredients. Cover and chill for an hour. Serve with grilled chicken, fish or pork.

Apple-Berry Salsa

A colorful, sweet and crunchy salsa.

2 medium Granny Smith apples, peeled, cored and chopped
1 pint strawberries, hulled and sliced
1 kiwifruit, peeled and chopped
1/2 cup chopped walnuts
3 tbsps. brown sugar
3 tbsps. apple jelly
Zest and juice from 1 navel orange

In a medium bowl, combine apples, strawberries, kiwifruit, walnuts, brown sugar and apple jelly. Toss to combine.

Stir in the orange zest and orange juice. Serve with toasted tortillas dusted with cinnamon or with pork.

Three Berry Salsa

**A sweet and slightly tangy salsa. The habanero adds
a bite that follows the sweet taste.**

1 pint blueberries, rinsed
1 pint strawberries, rinsed, hulled and quartered
1 pint raspberries, rinsed
1/4 cup sugar
1/4 cup minced sweet onion (1015 or Vidalia)
2 tbsps. raspberry vinegar
1 tsp. freshly ground black pepper
1 habanero, seeded and minced
1/4 cup sliced toasted almonds

In a large bowl, combine the berries, sugar, onion, vinegar, black pepper and habanero. Mix well, cover and refrigerate for at least an hour. Just before serving, stir in toasted almonds. Serve chilled with poultry or pork.

Rhubarb-Raspberry Salsa

A sweet-tart salsa with a wonderful touch of fresh mint.

2 cups whole almonds
6 tbsps. butter, melted
4 tbsps. sugar
2 tbsps. ground cinnamon
1 pound rhubarb stalks, peeled and sliced into ½-inch pieces
2 cups whole raspberries
1 tsp. lemon juice
1 cup sugar
3 tbsps. cornstarch
1/4 tsp. salt
1/4 cup fresh mint leaves, torn

Preheat oven to 350F.

In a large bowl, toss the almonds with the melted butter, using your hands to ensure all almonds are well coated. Add the sugar and cinnamon and continue mixing with your hands until all almonds are evenly coated. Spread almonds onto a baking sheet, pouring any leftover sugar mixture on top. Bake for 20 minutes. Remove from oven (keep oven on) and allow to cool completely. (Almonds can be made in advance and stored in an airtight container for several weeks.)

In a large bowl, combine rhubarb, raspberries, lemon juice, sugar, cornstarch and salt. Stir well to combine and pour into a baking dish. Bake at 350F for 20 minutes, or until mixture is bubbly, resembling a pie filling.

Allow fruit to cool to room temperature. Just before serving, stir in the toasted almonds and fresh mint. Serve with blue corn tortilla chips, chicken, pork or fish.

Blueberry Salsa

A beautiful, sweet and slightly spicy salsa.

2-1/2 cups blueberries, rinsed and chopped
3/4 cup minced red onion
1 red bell pepper, diced
2 jalapeños, seeded and minced
3 tbsps. finely chopped cilantro
Juice of 2 limes
1 tsp. salt

Combine all ingredients and refrigerate for at least an hour. Serve with tortilla chips or grilled fish.

Summer Salsa

A great salsa to combine some of the best flavors of the summer.

1 cup chopped fresh pineapple
1 cup chopped cantaloupe
1 cup chopped honeydew melon
1 cup chopped mango
3 kiwifruit, peeled and chopped
1/2 cup chopped fresh strawberries
3 tbsps. chopped fresh mint
2 tbsps. fresh lime juice

Combine all ingredients in a bowl. Stir gently. Chill for at least an hour. Serve with tortilla chips, crackers, fish, shellfish or chicken.

Orange Pomegranate Salsa

A wonderful sweet salsa for the autumn months.

1 large pomegranate
2 large oranges, peeled, seeded and chopped
1 large tomato, peeled, seeded and diced
4 green onions, sliced lengthwise into long thin strips
1 jalapeño, seeded and minced
Juice of 1 lime
1 tbsp. minced fresh cilantro
1/2 tsp. ground cumin

Break the pomegranate apart to release the seeds. Discard membranes and skin. Drain seeds and pat dry on paper towels.

In a medium bowl, combine the pomegranate seeds with the remaining ingredients. Stir well. Cover and chill for at least 2 hours. Serve with blue corn tortilla chips, fish, ham or pork.

Tangy Cherry Marsala Salsa

A sweet, tart salsa with a hint of fresh rosemary.

2 cups marsala wine
1/2 cup dried tart cherries
12-oz. bag frozen cranberries
12-oz. bag frozen dark cherries, halved
1 cup packed golden-brown sugar
1 tsp. minced fresh rosemary
1/2 tsp. ground allspice

Combine marsala and dried cherries in a saucepan. Bring to a boil and cook, uncovered, until the mixture is reduced to about 2/3 cup (about 8 minutes). Add remaining ingredients and return to a boil, stirring occasionally. Reduce heat to medium, cover and simmer until the cranberries burst and the mixture thickens.

Transfer to a bowl and refrigerate for at least 3 hours. Serve with poultry or pork.

Red Wine Pear & Raspberry Salsa

A full-bodied dessert salsa.

2 cups cabernet sauvignon
4 Bosc pears, peeled, cored and halved
½ cup Beaujolais wine
1 tbsp. heavy cream
2 cups fresh raspberries, divided
1/2 cup sugar
1/2 tsp. ground ginger
Dash of ground nutmeg
2 oz. white chocolate chips, melted

In a small, heavy saucepan over medium-low heat, bring cabernet sauvignon to a simmer. Add pears, cover and poach for about 15 minutes. Remove pears from wine and set aside to cool, discarding wine.

In the same saucepan, combine the Beaujolais, cream, 1 cup of the raspberries, the sugar and the ginger and nutmeg. Bring to a boil. Reduce heat and simmer 3 minutes, stirring constantly. Press mixture through a sieve to remove seeds. Allow to cool.

Cut poached pears into medium dice and place in serving bowl. Add remaining 1 cup raspberries and the raspberry sauce. Stir gently to combine. Just before serving, drizzle with melted white chocolate. Serve with thin chocolate wafers or gingersnaps.

Pineapple Chipotle Salsa

A smoky, sweet and spicy salsa.

2 cups fresh pineapple chunks
8 chipotle peppers in adobo sauce, diced
2 tbsps. dark rum
¼ cup pineapple juice
¼ cup Coco Lopez cream of coconut
Juice of 1 lime

Combine all ingredients in a medium bowl and toss to combine. Serve chilled with chicken, ham or pork.

Curried Apricot Salsa

A sweet, chunky salsa with a taste of India.

1 tsp. curry powder
2 cups diced apricot
1/4 cup diced red bell pepper
1/4 cup diced yellow bell pepper
1/4 cup diced red onion
1/4 tsp. salt

In a large skillet over low heat, toast the curry powder until fragrant, about 30 seconds. Remove from heat. Add remaining ingredients and stir until well blended. Serve warm with pork or ch1cken.

Mandarin Orange Salsa

A sweet and slightly smoky salsa. The optional habanero adds a touch of spice.

1 cup canned mandarin oranges, drained
4 chipotle peppers in adobo sauce
1/2 cup roughly chopped white onion
1/2 cup sugar
1/4 cup apple cider vinegar
2 garlic cloves, roughly chopped
Juice of 1 large navel orange
Zest of 1 large navel orange
1 tsp. orange extract
1 habanero, roughly chopped, optional

Combine all ingredients in a blender and process until smooth.

Serve with tortilla chips or pour over cream cheese and serve with gingersnaps.

Warm Raspberry Chipotle Salsa

A sweet, tangy salsa with a hint of smoked peppers.

1 tbsp. safflower oil
2 cups raspberries
4 chipotle peppers in adobo sauce, diced
2 cloves garlic, minced
1/4 cup raspberry vinegar
1 tsp. sugar
1/8 tsp. salt
1/8 tsp. black pepper

In a large skillet, warm the oil over medium-low heat. Add the raspberries and cook briefly, stirring, until berries begin to soften. Add the remaining ingredients and cook, stirring constantly, until warmed through. Serve immediately with tortilla chips or fish.

Sweet & Spicy Salsa

A sweet, fruity salsa with a touch of spice.

1 passion fruit, peeled and roughly chopped
1 pint strawberries, sliced
1 cup fresh pineapple chunks
1 cup peeled, pitted and diced fresh mango
1 cup peeled and diced papaya
1 cup red grapes, halved
1 serrano pepper, seeded and minced
1 tbsp. sugar
1 tbsp. mint leaves, chopped

Puree the passion fruit in a blender and pour into a large bowl. Add remaining ingredients and stir gently to combine. Chill until needed. Serve with cinnamon tortilla chips or grilled fish.

Berry Peppered Pear Salsa

A perfect combination of spicy and sweet.

3 pears, peeled, cored and cut into small dice
1 cup sweet white wine
1/2 cup raspberry vinegar
Juice of 1 lime
3 serrano peppers, minced
1 jalapeño pepper, minced
1 pint fresh raspberries, halved if they are large
1 pint fresh blackberries, halved if they are large
1 tsp. peeled and minced fresh ginger
3/4 tsp. crushed red pepper flakes

In a medium, deep nonreactive bowl, combine pears with wine, vinegar and lime juice. Either tie the peppers up in a cheesecloth sachet or place them in a tea infuser and add to the pears. Cover and refrigerate for at least 8 hours or overnight. Remove the sachet or infuser and discard the peppers. Strain the pears and reserve 2 tablespoons of the liquid.

Return the marinated pears to the bowl and add the raspberries and blackberries; stir gently to combine and set aside.

In a small bowl, combine reserved liquid, ginger and crushed red pepper flakes. Pour over fruit. Stir gently to combine. Serve immediately or cover and refrigerate. Serve with chicken, pork or tortilla chips.

Spicy Orange Salsa

This spicy bright-orange salsa makes an attractive addition to any hors d'oeuvre menu.

1/4 cup water
Juice and zest of 1 orange
3 tbsps. freshly squeezed lemon juice
2 carrots, roughly chopped
3 cloves garlic, roughly chopped
2 tbsps. chopped white onion
1 habanero pepper, stemmed
1 tsp. salt
1 tsp. brown sugar
1/4 tsp. ground ginger

Combine ingredients in a blender and process until smooth. Serve with tortilla chips or gingersnaps.

Raspberry Avocado Salsa

Sweet raspberries combined with the mellow flavor of ripe avocado create a wonderful accompaniment to any dish.

1 poblano chile
2 tbsps. safflower oil
1 shallot, minced
3 tbsps. raspberry vinegar
3 tbsps. poppyseeds
2 tbsps. sugar
1 large avocado, peeled, pitted and diced
2 cups fresh raspberries
1 tbsp. lemon juice

In the open flame of a gas burner or under a preheated broiler, roast the poblano, turning occasionally until blackened on all sides. Transfer chile to a bowl and cover with a plate. Allow to cool for at least 20 minutes.

While poblano is cooling, heat the oil in a small skillet over medium-high heat. Add the shallot and saute for about a minute, stirring frequently. Lower the heat to medium and stir in the raspberry vinegar, poppyseeds and sugar. Continue cooking for 3 minutes, stirring constantly. Remove from the heat and allow to cool.

Remove the poblano chile from the bowl and rub away the burned peel. Stem, seed and coarsely chop the chile and place in a medium bowl. Gently stir in the avocado, raspberries and lemon juice. Add the cooled vinegar mixture and fold together to combine.

Serve with tortilla chips, chicken or fish.

Cranberry-Pear Salsa

**A sweet cold-weather salsa that will add color
and flavor to any meal.**

1/2 cup maple syrup
1/4 cup apple cider vinegar
1/3 cup golden raisins
1/4 cup thinly sliced crystallized ginger
¼ cup thinly sliced white onion
1 garlic clove, thinly sliced
1 tsp. mustard seeds
1/2 tsp. ground red pepper
3 firm Bosc pears, peeled, cored and chopped
1/2 cup fresh or frozen cranberries

In a medium saucepan over medium-high heat, bring the maple syrup and vinegar to a boil. Reduce heat to medium. Add the raisins, ginger, onion, garlic, mustard seeds and red pepper. Mix well.

Stir in the pears and cook for about 15 minutes, or until the pears are soft and just beginning to lose their shape. Add cranberries and cook an additional 5 minutes (longer if adding directly from the freezer), or until cranberries begin to pop. Serve warm with chicken, turkey, ham or pork.

POSTRES SALSAS
(DESSERT SALSAS)

• • • • • • •

Sweet Thai Salsa

A very sweet and slightly spicy banana-based salsa.

3 tsps. Asian sesame oil
2 bananas, peeled and halved lengthwise
2/3 cup chopped golden raisins
1/4 cup chopped cilantro
2 tsps. grated lemon zest
1 tsp. chili oil

In a skillet over high heat, heat sesame oil and brown bananas, turning frequently, about 8 minutes. Remove from heat and allow bananas to cool enough to be handled, then roughly chop bananas. In a serving bowl, combine bananas with remaining ingredients.

Serve warm or chilled with gingersnaps or other cookies; may also be served with pork or chicken.

Pina Colada Macadamia Salsa

**A very sweet dessert salsa with the flavors
of the Caribbean islands.**

2 squares milk-chocolate almond bark
2 cups macadamia nuts, divided
1/2 cup shredded coconut
1/2 cup fresh pineapple wedges
1/2 cup diced mango
1/2 cup diced papaya
1/2 cup Coco Lopez cream of coconut
1/2 cup pineapple juice
1/4 cup Malibu rum

In the top of a double boiler or a heatproof bowl set over simmering water, melt the almond bark squares.

Spread 1 cup of the macadamia nuts on a baking sheet lined with wax paper. Pour the chocolate over the nuts to coat them evenly and set aside to cool.

Crush the remaining 1 cup of nuts coarsely and set aside.

In a large bowl, combine coconut, pineapple, mango, papaya and chocolate-covered nuts.

In a medium bowl, combine Coco Lopez, pineapple juice, rum and the remaining 1 cup crushed macadamia nuts. Pour Coco Lopez mixture on top of coconut-fruit mixture and stir gently to combine. Serve with vanilla wafers, chocolate wafers or angel food cake.

Banana Flambé Salsa

This flaming dessert salsa will make an impressive end to any special meal.

6 oz. semisweet chocolate chips
6 tbsps. Galliano liqueur, divided
1 tbsp. milk
1 tbsp. sugar
1 tbsp. com syrup
1/8 tsp. cinnamon
4 ripe but firm bananas, coarsely diced
1 cup fresh cherries, stemmed and pitted
1/2 cup flaked coconut

In the top of a double boiler, combine the chocolate chips, 4 tbsps. of the Galliano, milk, sugar, corn syrup and cinnamon. Cook, stirring occasionally, until chocolate is melted and mixture is smooth.

In a flameproof serving bowl, combine bananas, cherries and coconut.

In a small saute pan over medium-high heat, warm remaining 2 tablespoons Galliano. When liqueur is very hot, pour it over the chocolate and fruit mixture and light immediately for flambé effect. Serve with banana chips, angel food cake or gingersnaps or as a topping for ice cream.

Toffee Fruit Salsa

**Sweet and crunchy, this salsa is sure
to be a toffee-lover's dream.**

6 oz. semisweet chocolate chips
6 tbsps. Frangelico liqueur
1 tbsp. com syrup
1 tbsp. sugar
1 tbsp. milk
1 cup crushed Heath bars
1 cup cubed fresh pineapple, drained and patted dry
1 pint fresh strawberries, stemmed and quartered, drained and patted dry
Small can mandarin oranges, drained and patted dry

In the top of a double boiler or in a heatproof bowl over simmering water, combine chocolate chips, Frangelico, corn syrup, sugar and milk. Stir constantly until chocolate melts and mixture is smooth. Remove from heat. Allow to cool slightly and stir in crushed Heath bars.

In a serving bowl, combine pineapple, strawberries and mandarin oranges. Pour chocolate mixture over fruit and stir gently to combine. Serve with gourmet vanilla wafers or other cookies.

Cherry Cordial Salsa

This rich, sweet dessert salsa presents the wonderful flavors of chocolate and cherries in a new way.

12 oz. double-chocolate chips
4 tbsps. Amaretto liqueur
4 tbsps. corn syrup
3 tbsps. heavy cream
2 tbsps. grenadine
1 tbsp. sugar
1-1/2 cups fresh cherries, stemmed and seeded (some cherries should be halved while some should remain whole)
1/2 cup coarsely chopped dried apricots
1/2 cup coarsely chopped dried pineapple
6 oz. white-chocolate chips

In the top of a double boiler or a heatproof bowl set over simmering water, warm double-chocolate chips until melted and smooth. Stir in Amaretto, corn syrup, cream, grenadine and sugar. Stir constantly until mixture is well-blended and smooth. Remove from heat.

In a serving bowl, combine cherries, apricots, pineapple and white-chocolate chips. Pour dark-chocolate sauce over fruit mixture and stir gently to combine. Serve with gourmet wafers, angel food cake or as a topping for ice cream.

Rocky Road Salsa

**This rich, sweet, dessert salsa combines many sinful
ingredients into one delicious salsa.**

1 cup semisweet chocolate chips
4 tbsps. Grand Marnier
4 tbsps. corn syrup
1 tbsp. sugar
1 tbsp. heavy cream
1/2 cup chopped walnuts
1 cup miniature marshmallows
1/2 cup milk-chocolate chips

In the top of a double boiler or a heatproof bowl set over simmering water, melt the semisweet chocolate chips, stirring constantly, until chocolate is smooth and creamy. Stir in the Grand Marnier, corn syrup, sugar and heavy cream.

In a medium bowl, combine walnuts, marshmallows and milk-chocolate chips. Pour chocolate sauce over walnut mixture and stir to combine.

Just before serving, microwave salsa for 30 seconds, or until marshmallows melt. Stir well to swirl in melted marshmallows. Serve with gingersnaps, vanilla wafers or as a topping for ice cream.

Brandied Berry Chocolate Salsa

A rich, sweet and smoky dessert salsa.

2 cups fresh raspberries
2 cups fresh strawberries, hulled and halved
2 cups brandy
1/2 cup sugar
12-oz. package semisweet chocolate chips
2 tbsps. corn syrup
1 tbsp. heavy cream
1 tbsp. sugar
2 chipotles in adobo sauce, finely chopped

In a large bowl, combine raspberries, strawberries, brandy and sugar. Cover and refrigerate at least 3 hours. When ready to serve, drain the berries and let sit to come to room temperature.

In the top of a double boiler or in a heatproof bowl set over simmering water, heat the chocolate chips, stirring constantly, until melted and smooth. Add corn syrup, heavy cream, sugar and chipotles; continue stirring until heated through.

Pour sauce over berries and serve warm with cinnamon tortilla chips or as a topping to ice cream.

Glossary

Ancho chiles: Dried chile peppers 3 to 4 inches long, deep reddish-brown to almost black, leathery and wrinkled in appearance, with broad shoulders and pointed tips. Mild-flavored, they are the dried version of the poblano pepper. They can be ground into powder or reconstituted by soaking in warm water. Found in Texas and Southwestern supermarkets and in Hispanic markets, spice markets and specialty stores elsewhere, as well as online.

Capers: The flower bud of a plant native to the Mediterranean and parts of Asia. Sun-dried and usually pickled in brine, they are widely available; look for them in supermarkets with the olives and other similar condiments.

Chili oil: Vegetable oil infused with hot red chiles, available in the Asian section of most supermarkets.

Chipotle chiles in adobo sauce: Jalapeños that have been smoked and canned in a thick, smoky, vinegary tomato-based sauce. Smoky-hot in flavor, they can be found in the Hispanic-foods section of most supermarkets.

Cilantro: Also known as fresh coriander, it is a relative of the parsley family, with broad, lacy leaves similar to those of Italian parsley and a pronounced flavor. It's easily found in the produce sections of most grocery stores.

Coco Lopez: Sweetened cream of coconut, it can be found at liquor stores and many grocery stores that carry cocktail ingredients.

Frangelico: A sweet, hazelnut-flavored liqueur from Italy, found in most liquor stores.

Galliano: Anise-flavored liqueur from Italy with a rich golden color from Italy, found in most liquor stores.

Grenadine: A sweet, red pomegranate-flavored syrup, found in many grocery stores and most liquor stores with other cocktail ingredients.

Habanero chiles: Small, blistering-hot bright-orange or bright-red chiles also known as Scotch bonnets. With a fruity flavor and aroma and a "back-of-the-throat" heat, they pair well with fruits and sweet flavors. They can be found in the produce sections of Texas and Southwestern supermarkets, Hispanic and Caribbean markets and other specialty markets specializing in exotic produce.

Hoisin sauce: A thick, dark-reddish-brown, predominantly sweet sauce used extensively in Chinese cooking. Available in the Asian section of most larger supermarkets and at Asian markets and specialty grocers.

Jalapeño chiles: Probably the most commonly known chiles in the U.S., these are medium-sized chiles with a heat level that can vary widely; some jalapeños are bred to be very mild, while others can be rather hot. They are usually sold when dark green, though if left to ripen on the plant they will turn a rich bright red and are sometimes sold that way. They are sold both fresh and pickled (packed in jars or cans); when jalapeños are called for in this book, fresh jalapeños are indicated unless otherwise noted.

Jicama: A large, bulbous root vegetable with a dirty-brown skin and a white, crisp flesh, it has a sweet, nutty flavor and can be served raw or cooked. Available in the produce sections of many supermarkets.

Kosher salt: A coarse-grained salt that is free of all additives. Preferred by many chefs for its texture and purity, kosher salt can be found in almost all supermarkets and in stores that stock baking supplies or kosher foods.

Marsala: A sweet Sicilian wine fortified with brandy, available in liquor stores.

New Mexico red chiles: Mild, dried dark-brown or black chiles 4 to 6 inches long. Their shiny, leathery skin has fewer wrinkles than the ancho; their shoulders are slimmer and their heat level higher as well. Found in many supermarkets and specialty stores and most Hispanic markets.

Nopales/nopalitos: The wide, flat, oval pads or paddles of the prickly pear cactus, nopales have a mild flavor some liken to that of green beans. When cut into small strips, they are called nopalitos. Nopales are sold in Hispanic markets and specialty produce markets. The fresh pads are usually sold trimmed of their long spines and shorter stickers, but be sure to examine them before you handle them in case a few lingering little stickers are left; any remaining should be carefully trimmed away before cooking. Nopalitos are also sold canned or jarred.

Pasilla chiles: Six to 8 inches long and about 1 inch in diameter, these long, skinny and pointed dried chiles have a rich, hot flavor and are a common ingredient in Mexican sauces and moles. Also known as chiles negros, they are the dried form of the chilaca chile and can be found in some supermarkets and many Hispanic grocery stores as well as online.

Passion fruit: Small, round tropical fruit native to Brazil. From March through September, this fruit can be found in most supermarkets that carry a large selection of produce.

Pinenuts: Small, light-colored nuts, they can be found with other nuts in most supermarkets and in ethnic markets.

Poblano chiles: A large, shiny, dark-green fresh chile with a very rich flavor, they are widely available in specialty supermarkets.

Sea salt: This salt is produced by evaporating sea water and often has larger flakes than regular salt. Most supermarkets carry it.

Serrano chiles: Small, skinny, pointed dark-green or red fresh peppers. A good deal hotter than jalapeños, they are often substituted for jalapeños when more heat is wanted. Commonly found in Texas and Southwestern supermarkets and in Hispanic or specialty stores elsewhere.

Shallots: These small members of the onion family grows in cloves and have a brown or reddish-brown papery skin. Milder and more delicate than their relatives, onions and garlic, they are stocked near them in the produce sections of most supermarkets.

Tomatillos: Members of the nightshade family and thus a relative of the tomato, tomatillos are small, firm and green, with a thin, parchment-like inedible husk and a tart, bright flavor that hints of lemon and apple. A native of Mexico, they are found in most supermarkets in Texas and the Southwest and in Hispanic markets.

Working With Chiles

Most types of chile peppers are sold both fresh and dried, but the dried version typically goes by a different name from the fresh. Dried peppers can be ground into a powder for seasoning, but for use in salsas, they are typically split and deseeded, toasted in a dry skillet or on a comal (griddle) and then rehydrated in warm water before being chopped or pureed.

With all chiles, the heat is concentrated in the seeds and veins, which can be removed for a milder effect. The heat level s typically highest in the stem end of the pepper and decreases gradually toward the end or point of the pepper.

When working with the hotter peppers (or if you have sensitive skin), wear gloves to protect your skin and wash your hands thoroughly immediately after working with peppers. Be careful not to touch your eyes or other sensitive areas while working with chiles.

Consider other offerings in our line of acclaimed Texas & Southwestern cookbooks